Thérèse Yelverton

## Saint Augustine, Florida

Sketches of its history, objects of interest, and advantages as a resort for

health and recreation

Thérèse Yelverton

**Saint Augustine, Florida**
*Sketches of its history, objects of interest, and advantages as a resort for health and recreation*

ISBN/EAN: 9783337112806

Printed in Europe, USA, Canada, Australia, Japan

Cover: Foto ©Lupo / pixelio.de

More available books at **www.hansebooks.com**

# SAINT AUGUSTINE,

## FLORIDA.

SKETCHES OF ITS HISTORY, OBJECTS OF INTEREST, AND
ADVANTAGES AS A RESORT FOR HEALTH
AND RECREATION.

BY AN ENGLISH VISITOR.

WITH NOTES FOR NORTHERN TOURISTS ON ST. JOHN'S
RIVER, ETC.

PRINTED FOR
E. S. CARR, *St. Augustine*—C. DREW & CO., *Jacksonville, Fla.*
NEW YORK:
G. P. PUTNAM & SON.
1869.

THE TROW & SMITH
BOOK MANUFACTURING COMPANY,
46, 48, 50 GREENE ST., N. Y.

# SAINT AUGUSTINE.

A SKETCH BY AN ENGLISH VISITOR.

SAINT AUGUSTINE, the most ancient town of North America, is situated in Florida, upon a narrow slip of land formed by the St. Johns river on the one side and the ocean upon the other.

Florida was discovered in 1512 by Ponce de Leon, a companion of Columbus; one of the enterprising adventurers of the sixteenth century.

At that period, when the love of the marvellous still held its sway equally over the lettered as over the untutored mind, there was a story prevalent, that away north beyond the West Indian Islands there was a land of Elysium, rich with fruits and flowers, and possessing a river in whose waters flowed the Elixir of Life, conferring perpetual youth and beauty on whomsoever should lave in or drink of them. Inspired by this brilliant legend, and in hopes of making a discovery which should far outreach that of Columbus, Ponce de Leon set sail from Porto Rico, and coming in sight of the Peninsula of Florida, and landing near the present site of St. Augustine in April, it is no wonder he believed he had realized the fable of the promised land in this

Elysium of constantly renewed bliss of youth and beauty. For nothing could look more like a paradise than Florida in April. Then he beheld it bathed in balmy light, redolent in fruit, flowers, and sunshine. Not only flowers, shrubs, and undergrowth by millions were in bloom, but the very forest trees fill the air with the fragrance of their blossoms. The palmetto spreads its fanlike leaves to waft the breeze, the date palm waves its majestic plumes in the translucent blue air, and the feathery acacia and chaporell tremble to the gentle kiss of wooing zephyrs.

The magnolia reflects the glowing sunshine upon its glossy leaves and contrasts its creamlike flowers with the radiant scarlet of the pomegranate. The golden oranges hang in tempting clusters among their fresh green leaves, while here and there peep out their scented blossoms.

The lilies, in their grace and purity, as of old, put to shame "Solomon in all his glory:" sleeping on the placid water, cushioned on velvet leaves, or dancing in the air highly suspended on their spiral stems, or humbly hiding in mossy nooks and fairy dells; then appearing as the imperial oriflamme, the Fleur de Lis of France, clothed in royal purple or gorgeous as the scarlet trumpet lily, dazzling with its glory.

Not only the lilies bloom perennially in this discovered land of Ponce de Leon; the eglantine, in its tender embrace of all whom it can reach, the rose, the verbena, and jessamine entwine their fragrance and their foliage. The vine clings with delicate tendrils round every projecting rugged trunk that needs a shade.

The " best loved West Wind " sighs through the pine barrens with a sweet and hallowed tone, like the voices of our loved and lost ones whispering us from the Spirit Land. The red-bird radiates prisms of light from his flaming wing, and when the heavens, which are always blue, are bespangled with stars, the air is filled with showers of fire-flies dashing to and fro like brilliant heavenly messengers, skimming and floating on the vast expanse of ethereal vault. If they are not angels, Ponce de Leon might have taken them for such, bearing to earth glad tidings from their celestial home above, illuminating the orange-groves; lighting up the dark cypress and ancient cedars, hung with sepulchral moss, as though the wood nymphs and forest sprites were holding high carnival. All this and more than this of beauty that pen fails to describe, Ponce de Leon must have beheld when he landed in Florida in April. It may be seen to this day by every visitor to this enchanting spot.

He might easily have pictured in the semi-lake-like waters of the St. Johns river the realization of his day dream, the Elixir of Life.

Flowing soft and silvery through bankless flats of luxuriant foliage, draped with the funereal moss hanging from the evergreen oak, or the pine and orange alternate laving in its brim: now spreading out to a placid lake where the stately pelican floats at lonely leisure—anon closing in to the limits of a stream, every leaf and spray reflected in its clear bosom, and the pink crane in solemn meditation. The waters, having a soft, sweet taste, might well have been mistaken by Ponce de Leon for Elixir, and doubtless he drank it by the quart in the true American fashion. But alas! the proof of the pudding was in the eating, or drinking in this case: he grew neither young nor handsome. *Qui sa ?* as the natives say, if this may not be the original cause of the great quantity of water consumed by Americans: even now they grow not younger, but considerably yellower; for quarts of ice water and pounds of hot bread would destroy the beauty of Venus herself.

Thus Ponce de Leon became disgusted with his paradise, and finding the native Indians fierce and implacable, he returned to Spain a disappointed man.

In his hopes and aspirations he was followed by other Spaniards, Narvaez and De Soto.

But the first permanent settlement was effected by the French in the reign of Charles the Ninth, after the Saint Bartholomew and during the Coligny troubles.

The Huguenots obtained permission to exile

to America, where they are still traceable in some of the Southern States, who, nevertheless, in their own hour of discord and disunion, did not allow those who dissented to retire, but rather to force them by pains and penalties to succumb to the new established order of affairs. So true it is that those who have been oppressed are ever the first to turn oppressors. And this fact should act as a warning in the present emancipation of slaves.

The French had scarcely enjoyed the results of their freedom and their labors in building a fort near Saint Augustine, when Menendez, the Spanish commander arrived from Spain, with powers to take possession of Florida and govern it in the king's name. He surprised the Huguenots by night, and entered the fort during a heavy thunder-storm. They, never anticipating any attack save by sea, had left their fort on the land side almost unguarded, and were most of them butchered in their sleep. Some few escaped into the woods, but were eventually obliged by famine to surrender. They were given their choice to renounce their faith or meet their death. They unanimously chose the martyr's fate, and were butchered in cold blood, "Dying as their fathers died, for the faith their foes denied." Their exile, toil, and labor had not saved them from the fate of Coligny; they had flown from their homes in France only to rush into the jaws of Spanish Inquisitors.

The escutcheon of Menendez, the great Spanish commander, is traced in blood, and the foundation-stone of Saint Augustine which he laid is saturated with the gore of these brave and undaunted victims to religious tyranny and persecution.

Blood having been so cruelly spilt at the baptism as it were of Saint Augustine, seems to have flowed freely through its walls and towers for three centuries of its history. For it has been watered with its own blood from its very birth to its hoary age, more than any city on this continent. It has suffered more ravages of fire, sword, and famine than any other city, and its inhabitants have acknowledged more foreign rulers and various flags than any other city.

It is necessary to bear this in mind in forming any opinion of the present occupants of Saint Augustine. Indeed, in coming to any ethnological, metaphysical or moral conclusion as to American character, it is essential to note the various causes which have tended to populate this vast and magnificent country.

It is not a country that has been conquered or overrun by a stronger people. The native Indians have retired before the white man, leaving little trace behind. From the earliest date we find it the sanctum of those brave men driven from their homes by persecution—of the Huguenots, who had sealed their belief with their heart's blood. The dauntless followers of Ribault, the first settlers of this little colony, were the heroic victims of another St. Bartholomew. Historians disagree about the number who fell, but it was doubtless from three to four hundred.

Religious and political persecution at home, have both tended to establish this great Nation more than any other cause.

But for that, the Pilgrim Fathers would never have landed on the wild New England shore, nor the gallant Cavalier, South Carolina and Virginia. Nor would the Irish and Germans have found their way to the prairies of the West, save for political persecution at home.

The penal laws against the Irish in the last and beginning of the present century, have been a prolific cause of immigration, and have done more to depopulate Ireland and colonize Western America than any other cause.

But where a man lives under a ban and is branded for his religious or political opinions for years; where the future is robbed of those radiant tints which so dazzle and delight in our forward gaze, which make anticipation the secret charm of our existence, the guiding star and leading magnate which drives us on to exertion, stronger effort and enterprise—when hope folds her wings and sits brooding under the spurning feet of persecution—the human heart casts abroad in search of a spot where it may be free; free to expand and glory in its thoughts and aspirations; free to worship in a temple or on the mountain-top. Such a spot was found in the benignant continent of America. She lay with her fair wide bosom open to take in all who mourned and were afflicted. To gather them in her genial embrace, and make them welcome to her fold. The per-secuted patriot, loving his country more than his own happiness, borne down in his zeal to stem the purple tide of tyranny and usurpation; the religious enthusiast, braving the faggot and in-strument of torture for a conscientious principle of faith, and bidding defiance to inquisitors and hell's power to pain, rather than relinquish the right to worship from his heart's pure inspiration; the woe-begone Irish mother, with her brood of starvelings; the sullen father, whose spirit is nigh crushed to bitterness and evil from the long weight of his wrongs; the timid young girl, whose early lines of beauty are mingled with those of care—all come trooping with eager steps to the Land of the Free. To the land of corn, and fruits and flowers. To the land of every clime, of every sky; every temperature for every race. To all who are overburdened and oppressed she extends her snowy arms from the tops of her giant Rocky Mountains, and steps out on her Californian feet, clad in sandals of gold, to give them welcome. She spreads her flower-enamelled lap over vast prairies to the weary and worn; and the shelter

of her pine forests to each and every one. God's
mercy goeth not out of reach, and his dew falls
on the feverish eyelids of those who weep.

To the toilsome, patiently enduring German,
driven at last to bay by tyrannical exaction on
his down-trodden liberty, she offers her glowing
homesteads, with independent, healthful labor—
her waving corn-fields and lowing kine, wood
and water in reach of every hand; her seas, having a thousand miles of coast, cast up their ma-
rine fruits and store with prodigal munificence.

Beautiful, generous land, offering every gift
to man that man's heart can rightly desire.
Surely Ponce de Leon might have been satisfied
with his portion of the discovery.

Such, however, is human nature. He had set
his affections upon a particular object, viz., youth
and beauty à *perpetueté ;* and not realizing that,
all the rest seemed unavailing to satisfy this
craving.

The same thing happens to this day on the
same spot, where the sweet and bitter orange
still abound. The fig, peach, lemon, and pomegranate refresh the eye, and cool the palate.
Northern travellers are grumbling every day
because they cannot procure dirty *tap-water*, and
purchase lake ice. Ice-water is an American
mania, an anti-hydrophobia sort of disease; and
it is quite certain, if there is not a good supply of ice-water in heaven, they will all peti-

tion St. Peter to be allowed to return to New
York.

They all repined because Wenham Lake ice
could not be raised in Florida; every other
growth was in vain. Ponce de Leon being disgusted because the water did not perpetuate
youth and beauty, was yet less unreasonable than
these Northern travellers.

Hence youth and beauty *à perpetueté, can not*
be offered as one of the productions of Florida.
Nevertheless, we can, on the authority of the
historian from whom we have obtained the dates
and facts relating to this portion of the country,
go so far as to state that at the period of the
evacuation by the Spaniards, numbers of the inhabitants left the city who were over one hundred years of age; and there still lives in the
town of St. Augustine a negro who is said to be
one hundred and eighteen.

Apropos of beauty, where all nature is so
lovely, it would be an anomaly for human nature
to form an exception.

As regards all those adjuncts which make our
exterior life enjoyable, Florida abounds in a
larger share than any climate I have visited;
and St. Augustine, with her cool sea breeze and
cloudless sun, is doubtless the Eden of Florida.
Had Ponce de Leon only had the good fortune,
like his great forefather, to espy an Eve mirror-
ing herself in the blue waters of the bay, and

enamored of the reflection, he would no doubt have followed suit and not only proclaimed it a paradise but inhabited by Peris. So it is that "Man never is but always to be blest." He, finding the Indian squaws the reverse of Venuses, and the men more like unto Mars, returned, we are told, disconsolate to Spain. In 1580, shortly after the death of Menendez, St. Augustine was attacked by the celebrated English Admiral, Sir Francis Drake. But after some ineffectual attempts to dislodge the Spaniards from the fortifications which they had established there, he abandoned the siege, and sailed on his voyage.

About this period, the Franciscan missionaries came to this country, with the purpose of Christianizing the natives. They settled in St. Augustine, where they built the first church at the Indian village of Talmato, where the burying-ground remains to the present time, most interesting to visit, from the old Spanish tombs which remain almost perfect. They are constructed of the *Coquina* stone or shell, and bear a strong resemblance to some of the Egyptian sarcophagi or stone coffins. Some of them were cut out from a solid piece, the lid consisting of a large slab. Some were put together in slabs and partly buried in the earth. It is also interesting as the site of the first martyr to religious zeal, the first Franciscan monk. This order, the rivals of the Jesuits, in pioneering Christianity and civilization, were indefatigable in their endeavors to civilize the Indians, and for some time apparently succeeded. But there seems to be something in the nature of the red men of the forest which bids defiance both to religion and cultivation, and is incompatible with either.

Three centuries have now well nigh elapsed, of continued effort; but the Indian tribes remain as wild and primitive as the trees of their own forests.

It was in vain that the Padre Corpa, the foremost of the missionary band, rejoiced in the conversion of one of the chiefs with all his tribe. Having dared to lecture his new convert upon the unchristian number of his wives, his doom was passed. He was barbarously murdered at the foot of his own altar, as he was preparing to celebrated mass, by the chief and his tribe, the devoted Padre stipulating in his sublime agony only for sufficient time to perform the service, which was accorded, his executioners lying around whilst he prayed for their forgiveness for the last time, and gloating over their prey like famished wolves, and glaring upon him with the eyes of the hyena. No sooner was the service concluded and he turned to give them his benediction, than they rushed up him and tore him limb from limb, his head being the only portion of him ever found by his brethren.

This act alone was in itself a startling proof

that no sentiment of Christianity had ever entered their savage breasts and in all probability never would. The *spirit* of Christianity is incomprehensible to them.

The devoted missionaries, however, were not of this opinion. They steadily pursued their sacred calling, building over twenty churches and mission-houses through Florida. Their head house, the Franciscan Convent, is now the handsomest building in St. Augustine, having been renovated and turned into a barrack for the Union troops. It is still claimed as the property of the Church, and the matter is one of interminable litigation. The next handsomest building is the Convent of the Sisters of Mercy, which has recently been erected. The castle or fort, the most picturesque, was built in 1620, principally by the forced labor of the Indians, who, for sixty years, were compelled to work as servants to the Spaniards. This is more than the Americans have ever been able to make them do, even for themselves; for the Indians consider it an indignity to labor; and, up to the present day, neither argument, persuasive or forcible, has had the effect of inducing them to live otherwise than in the complete simplicity of unsophisticated nature. They will neither construct nor provide for the future. They will live upon the produce of the land, as provided by nature, and upon the animals which come within their power to destroy for food.

Any thing which we call improvement and cultivation, they are averse to ; and when pressed upon them, they retire further and further back to their fastnesses and mountains, but cannot be brought to adopt the ideas of the white man, or amalgamate with him in social intercourse. These were the primitive inhabitants of St. Augustine, then under the name of Talmato, when the Spaniards first took possession.

In 1665, the town of St. Augustine was again besieged and captured, in spite of the castle and fort, which was then octagon and flanked by round towers, still in existence.

This time the unfortunate little town was captured and destroyed by an English buccaneer, cruising upon his own account, in search of booty and adventure.

Upon these occasions, which appear to have been not unfrequent at poor St. Augustine, it was the custom of the inhabitants to retire into the fortress, carrying with them all their household goods which were portable, and leaving the town to the mercy of the invaders, or, in other words, to be ransacked and destroyed. It would therefore be difficult to determine at what precise period any particular part of St. Augustine was built.

After the retiring of the buccaneer, the unhappy inhabitants were beset by the sea on the other side, against whose encroachments they were obliged to build a sea-wall, the remains of which are still visible on Bay-street, much within the limits of the present one, constructed at a much later date, and now the fashionable promenade, being about four feet broad, and extending the whole way from the fort to the barracks—a distance of more than a mile. Admitting only of two abreast, it is naturally the favorite resort of lovers, who thus enjoy the sea-air and the picturesque little bay.

In 1681, the famous "Friend," William Penn, obtained, from Charles II. of England, a grant of land in Florida, which he strove to colonize— it is to be hoped, from his principles and character—by other means than by fire or sword, like most of the colonizers of this period. He did not interfere with St. Augustine.

But in 1702, England being at war with Spain, the colonies seized this opportunity to have another skirmish with little Spanish St. Augustine. The English, under Governor Moore, once more took possession of the town, driving the inhabitants into the fortress, which resisted the attack of the enemy. After remaining and devastating the place for a month, they were frightened away by the appearance, in the offing, of two ships, which they mistook for Spanish men-of-war. They at once prepared to decamp, and marched overland to Charleston, a distance of three hundred miles, burning all that was combustible before leaving.

The vicissitudes of the picturesque little town seem, about 1712, to have been varied by a famine, owing to the non-arrival of the vessels from Spain, carrying the usual supplies upon which they depended for their support. So that, after one hundred years' settlement, they were still unable to supply themselves with the necessaries of life, in a land abounding in fish, fowl, game, fruit, and vegetables. Still stranger to relate, at the present time, a century and a half later, almost every thing is supplied from the north, and northern energy and capital furnish much that is produced on the spot.

Spaniards were never good colonizers, and rarely did more than simply stagnate upon the country they took by conquest or otherwise. The *dolce far niente* is still prevalent in St. Augustine to the present time; and, having once had their orange-groves destroyed by some accidental frost, which had lost its way and come there, they consider this a sufficient reason for never planting or grafting any more. But war's waste and ravages were not at an end for St. Augustine, and seem never to have been; for at the period of the late war of Secession, she had to change hands three times.

In 1725, a party under Col. Palmer, from Charleston, made another incursion—the town falling a prey. They burned, killed, and destroyed, and then departed. Again, eight years later, Oglethorpe laid siege to the place in regular form, planting his batteries upon the island of Anastasia, and bombarding both fort and town therefrom. This was the most formidable siege which St. Augustine had ever sustained, and it lasted several months—the enemy having at length to retire, leaving the fort uncaptured. Previous to this, the fort had been put in a thorough state of defence. The ramparts had been heightened, bomb-proof vaults constructed, entrenchments thrown up, and ravelins projected. The fort then presented a formidable appearance, and, although upon a small scale, it was considered as impregnable as any in Europe. Events realized this supposition; for although Gen. Oglethorpe was considered one of the greatest commanders of that day, and although he displayed great talent and perseverance, sparing no expense or effort, the fort, then called San Juan, withstood him, and although subjected to more than a score of attacks, it never once yielded or fell into the hands of its besiegers. With the exception of again laying the town in ruins, and nearly starving out the garrison and inhabitants refuged in the fort, amounting to 2,500, Gen. Oglethorpe was no more successful than his predecessors, and had finally to abandon his position.

In spite of this failure, he with true British pertinacity made a détour by land, some two years later, and appearing with a large army

before the fort, with drums beating and flags
flying, dared the garrison to come out and give
battle. The Spaniards, believing "discretion to
be the better part of valor," and choosing to leave
*well alone*, declined the challenge: and the
haughty general had ignominiously to walk back
again to Charleston. Reflection would doubtless
come, on the 300 mile road, for British foot was
never set within the brave little fort until it was
ceded by treaty in 1763.

Slavery, even at this early period, was showing
itself the apple of discord of this distracted land.
The excuse or pretext for these continual attacks
was the accusation that the Spaniards inveigled
and retained slaves belonging to the British, and
they stormed the place with a view of recovering
them. Slavery was also the actual cause of the
long Floridian war which desolated the country
for so many years. And Slavery has, alas, del-
uged not only Florida but the whole of this fair
continent in blood. Pray heaven that this hydra-
headed monster in this last great struggle has
bled itself to death. Its history in peace or war
is written in human blood, not alone of the soldier
who perished at his post, to enforce barbarous
laws, or the wild Indian dyeing with his heart's
blood the green leaves of his hummuck, but of
helpless woman, screeching out her sad story under the lash of the tyrant. One breathes more
freely this delicious air, to know that these atro-

cities are at an end for ever; to believe that the worm corroding at the heart of the fairest land of God's creation is destroyed; that the great skeleton looming over her youthful beauty has crumbled to ashes, and that now she may ripen to maturity and perfection.

It is only just to say that Florida and St. Augustine prospered more under the 20 years which followed of British possession and rule, than she had done in the two hundred years of their predecessors.

The exports in indigo and turpentine rose to forty and fifty thousand pounds yearly.

There was no question now of starving to death in a land of plenty, as had been the case under the Spaniards. Barely, however, had the English obtained peaceable possession, and St. Augustine began to prosper, before the Declaration of American Independence took place, and placed them at daggers drawn with the United States; and the town was again made the *point d'appui* for the British forces against the American, and it was still her destiny to be kept in a state of trouble and warfare.

1784 saw this province of Florida re-ceded to Spain in pursuance of treaty between the two countries.

The singular mixture of the inhabitants at this time, and the strange confounding of tongues, must somewhat have resembled Babel. English,

Spanish, French, American, Indian, African, must have formed a curiously heterogeneous compound—a real pot-pourri of nationality.

Until 1812 the country continued to be harassed by the Americans constantly yearning for more territory. The King of Spain came to the sage conclusion "que le jeu ne vallait pas la chandelle," that the colony cost more than it was worth. He sold it to the United States for so many millions of dollars.

### PRESENT CONDITION.

Saint Augustine is therefore interesting to the moralist from its many and varied vicissitudes. To the antiquary from its antique remains of old Spanish customs and characteristics—its narrow streets, projecting balconies nearly reaching across and forming a constant shade—its verandas and remains of ancient porticos. The old Catholic Cathedral, with its quaint Moorish belfry and chime of bells, which, if properly played, as in the ancient days, would produce melodious sounds enough, but which now send forth the frequent call to prayer by being *rattled* with a *stick*. The Angelus, which is kept up in Saint Augustine, as in all Catholic countries, where the touching announcement of the Angel is softly pealed three times a day, is here rattled out. If the Angelus Domini was as uproarious as at St. Augustine, the Virgin would not have cared for a second visit.

On Sundays the Episcopalians, who have their pretty little semi-Gothic church on the opposite side of the square, are brought to a summary standstill in their devotion. The minister has usually arrived at the peroration of his sermon when the rub-a-dub-dub commences in the Cathedral. The congregation cannot hear another syllable to save their souls, and the ringing or rattling continues often for half an hour.

The fort is of course the chief object of interest in Saint Augustine, especially by moonlight, and there is not a more picturesque place anywhere. Like Melrose, it may be said, " Who would see Fort Marion right, should view it by the fair moonlight." Few spots are more mysteriously romantic. The fort was built to command both land and sea, with round towers at each corner; cannon mounted on the walls and ramparts. It is built entirely of the Coquina stone—a geological marvel in itself. It is formed of a concrete of small shells which centuries have massed together, forming a hard rock, but in which each shell is perfectly distinct and visible and sometimes complete as though they had been tightly glued together but yesterday. The whole structure, upon close examination, resembles one of those toy shell castles we purchase for children at seaports. Geologists and conchologists can probably determine how many centuries it has taken to amalgamate these myriads of tiny shells into one solid

mass of granite. It is quarried from Anastasia
Island.

Within the fort are shown chambers without light or air, which are said to have been
used by the Spanish Inquisition, from the fact of
a skeleton in chains being very recently found in
one of them. But unless one of the unfortunate
Huguenots who escaped the massacre of Menendez only to meet a more agonizing death, there
is no other record of religious intolerance. The
chambers have the usual appearance of the vault-
ed alcoves formed inside fortifications of this
period. One of these chambers has evidently
been the chapel, from the altar-stone still in good
preservation; and the holy water vessel used for
culinary purposes at the present time. Over the
gateway is the arms of Spain handsomely carved
in stone and quite perfect, and the inscription is
actually worthy of the proverbial bombast of the
Spaniard: "Don Fernando being King of Spain,
and the Field Marshal Don Alonzo Fernando
Herida being Governor and Captain General of
this place, St. Augustine of Florida and its prov-
inces, this fort was founded in the year 1756. The
works were directed by the Captain engineer Don
Pedro de Brazos y Gareuy." Round the fort is
a moat which can easily be filled from the sea, a
draw-bridge and portcullis, with other handsome
carvings surmounting them. The moat is surrounded by a broad diagonal wall, forming a

delightful promenade, always swept by a pleasant breeze.

The Atlantic Ocean rolls into a small bay formed by the mouth of the River Sebastian and Anastasia Island, whose sloping sands are as white as snow, and in some places as treachrous, sinking with the feet of the unwary explorist into quicksands. Beautiful shells of all descriptions are to be gathered on this beach, and the sail across the bay delightful. The porpoises and very good turtles luxuriate in it, and sometimes a shark. Plenty of good fish is caught in the bay, besides abundance of oysters and crabs. The fort appears to have changed names as often as owners, having been christened and re-christened San Juan, Saint Mark, and Marion, who it is to be supposed was a sinner, from dropping the title of Saint. There is more of mystery and romance attached to it than any other place in America,—probably on account of its Spanish occupation.

The frowning battlement and picturesque Moorish towers from whence we expect to see emerge the stately, dark-eyed Spaniard of Rembrantish line; the little chapel where the brown-cowled Franciscan told his breviary, regardless of the shrieks of his heretical victims in the adjacent vaults; the land breeze sighing over the pine barrens, might again hear the rattle of the chains and grinding of instruments of torture, said to have been found in this primitive Venetian prison. The roaring of the sea might recall the fierce bombardment from Anastasia Island, striking horror into the hearts of the ancient Augustinans huddled together within the fortress walls. Visitors linger in wonderment over the aperture so narrow, so high up in the stone vault, from which the wild and romantic Indian chief Coacouchee made his daring escape. His history is full of poetry, marvel and pathos. Scarcely had St. Augustine been ceded to the United States in 1821, when difficulties arose with the tribe of Indian warriors called Seminoles. The Spaniards and the English had lived on amicable terms with these tribes, and allowed them to retain peaceable possession of the best hummuck lands for their village.

### INDIAN HISTORY.

But the number of new settlers from the United States wishing to take possession of this beautiful and desirable land interfered greatly with the savage life of the Indians, who had no idea of being driven out of their forests and swamps, hunting-grounds and fishing-rivers and lakes, for the benefit of the new comers to grow their corn and cotton. Hence feuds arose, which did not end even with solitary murder and massacre, but brought about the Floridian War, which raged round St. Augustine for five or six years. Treaties were made to confine the wild-man within certain limits and boundaries. But the Indian, having ever considered this beautiful country as specially constructed for *his* benefit by the Great Spirit, could never be made to define any limits or bounds to his rovings; and was very apt to help himself to any crops or produce ready made to his hand. In fact, that impossible problem of the wild and civilized man existing together had to be solved, and the solution could be but one, by the disappearance of the former.

Coacouchee, the chief of the Seminoles, had come under a flag of truce to entertain what they denominate a "Talk," or negotiation. He had been retained a prisoner and confined in the Stone Chamber, from whence he made his wonderfully-daring escape through a port-hole, dropping himself some fifty feet.

Nothing can justify bad faith towards any people; but policy and necessity were the excuses set forth for this unjust detention of an ambassador, as it were, of peace—this abuse of the sacred rights of the flag of truce.

The United States had been at war five or six years without making any permanent conquest of this handful of erratic men, the tribe of the Seminoles. It was like warring against the wild-cat or the wind. Scoured from the land, they sheltered in the trees. Swept from the prairie, they were heard howling in the cypress swamp.

Driven to bay, they could swim the river or paddle their bark canoes across and back—an army would seek a ford or construct a pontoon bridge. Their unerring shots whistled through the pine branches, and their spears, like the tongues of snakes, hissed through the hummucks. There seemed no probability of vanquishing them by fair and honest warfare. A pitched battle was a farce. There was no enemy to be seen after the first round of musketry; it resembled a game at "Mother Bunch," who thinks to drive all her chickens before her whilst they are all scattered round and about.

Hence treachery as base as their own, was had recourse to; and they were finally partly forced, partly trepanned, partly cajoled in going farther West, and settling upon the hunting-grounds in Arkansas.

As recently as 1836, St. Augustine was kept in trepidation by the inroads of the Indians on various plantations in the environs, stealing negroes and carrying way crops, and perpetrating sundry atrocities in a similar fashion to the Indians West at this very day.

In regard to the enormity of these crimes, we should never lose sight of the peculiar position of the red and white man. The one is the natural inhabitant of the soil, living upon it as his birthright by the special dispensation of the Great Spirit, using all his gifts for his own benefit and that of his family. The white man is an intruder and encroacher, and the destroyer of his means of life.

Looking at the question from the Indian's most natural point of view, we might ask, what would be our conduct if some great, powerful nation were to appear and insist upon pulling down our factories and great cities to make pasture-lands? It is more than probable that a few barbarities would be committed by us, the most civilized people in the world.

There is, however, far more poetry about the red man than the black. Novelists have done much to idealize him, and associate him intimately with the dark pine forest and luxuriant hummuck. Agile, daring, fleet, and graceful; decked with the most brilliant trophies of the bird, beast, and fish, he could well become the hero of a theme for poets to sing, or novelists write wild stories of the flood and field. So well does he seem adapted to the country, and the country suited to him, that even at the present day, when inhabited by a white and mixed population, and his elastic tread has not bounded on his native soil or crushed the wild flowers and grass for more than twenty years, still, in traversing the vast, lonely glades of pine, or sailing on the smooth bosom of the St. Johns river, over-laden with dense foliage, one expects every moment to see his heron-plumed head-gear peer through the branches, or see the brushwood and undergrowth crushing under his agile spring, or hear his war-whoop echoing through the oak thickets.

The story of Coacouchee, as detailed by General Sprague, in his history of the Floridian War, is full of interest and poetry.

He was the son of a great chief called King Philip, and was thus an hereditary chief; added to which, he possessed in his own person all the requisites and qualifications of a great Indian leader. Shrewd, active, daring, and enduring, he was enabled to exercise commanding sway over his tribe, and appears to have won somewhat of the respect of his enemies. War to him was a pastime, and he delighted in the excitement as a hunter in the pursuit of game. Often when pursued to a deep swamp, he would turn and laugh, and jeer his pursuers, floundering with their arms and accoutrements through the mud and water, and enjoyed the sight of their disasters, whilst his own lithe figure skimmed easily through. He was as fleet as a deer, and as strong and fierce as a wolf. He was about twenty-eight years of age, slight in person, above the middle height, with a countenance bright, intelligent, playful, and attractive. After many hair-breadth escapes, and wonderful feats in flood and field, he was taken in the manner described, and confined in the fort, from whence he effected his escape as described, and succeeded in giving his captors a good deal of trouble after that. When he was again captured and brought into camp, he was informed that his liberty would only be restored to him upon his consent to immigrate with all his tribe to Arkansas. That he must send for his family, and all his warriors, who would be conveyed on the ship with him. Iron manacles were placed upon him to impress him with the futility of any attempt to escape, and to urge him to influence his own and other tribes to depart. For a time these irons seemed to eat into the very soul of the warrior, and deprive him of any spirit; his haggard and ghastly countenance bespoke the secret suffering of the wild animal caught in a trap; for to be chained, is the deepest degradation which can befall the free limbs of an Indian. Death in the open field, would be regarded as a boon in comparison. But by judicious talk and argument, he was finally brought to understand that his future in Arkansas would be free, and even more brilliant than in Florida, and that, as his own destiny in that direction was inevitable, he ought to encourage the other chiefs and tribes to join him. In these views he at length coincided, and messengers were sent bearing his authority to bring in the other chiefs, the women and children. He divested himself of his last and only garment, and sent it to his brother, with his earnest entreaties to yield himself, and spare him any longer the degradation of his chains.

The persuasiveness of this appeal could not be refused; the greater part of his people came in. The meeting between the tribe and their chief, was touching in the extreme.

As this is not a history of the Florida war, but a sketch of St. Augustine, it may be sufficient to mention that Coacouchee did emigrate, with a number of the warriors of his tribe, which once more left St. Augustine in peace.

When his irons were struck off, and he once more stood a free man, upon the vessel lying in Tampico bay, ready to bear him to his new home in Arkansas, he stood on the gangway gazing intently, and with lingering regret, on the loved land his foot might never press, on the land of his birth, the haunts of his childhood, the graves of his fathers. As the vessel heaved her anchor and put to sea, two large tears filled his dark eyes, and rolled down his bronzed cheeks. "I have taken farewell," he exclaimed, "of the last tree of my own land."

The existence of a Great Spirit was acknowledged by Coacouchee and by all Indians, and honored most devoutly by festivals, games, and dances, and medicine making. To this Great Spirit they believed themselves accountable for their acts.

Coacouchee's dream, as related to General Sprague, is full of the highest sentiment of poetry and spiritualized love and tenderness, which proves that the Indian, amidst all his ferocity, has yet a soul for high-toned chivalry, which has made him the hero of song and story. They were very opposite from the black race, who are neither graceful, symmetrical, handsome, simple or modest, and lacking all the dignity which marks the Indian chief—the picturesqueness and simplicity. The blacks are rather inclined to the ludicrous than the sublime. Coacouchee's story ran thus: "The day and manner of my death," he says, " are given out, so that whatever I may encounter I fear nothing. The Spirits of the Seminoles protect me, and the spirit of my twin sister, who died many years ago, watches over me. When I am laid in the earth I shall go to live with her. She died suddenly. I was out on a bear-hunt, and when seated by my camp-fire alone, I heard a strange noise, a voice that told me to go to her. The camp was some distance off, but I took my rifle and started. The night was dark and gloomy; the wolves howled about me. As I went from hummuck, sounds came often to my ear. I thought she was speaking to me. At daylight I reached the camp. She was dead! I sat down alone, and in the long gray moss hanging from the trees I heard strange sounds again. I felt myself moving, and went above into a new country where all was bright and beautiful. I saw clear water ponds, rivers, and prairies upon which the sun never set. All

3

was green; the grass grew high, and the deer
stood in the midst looking at me. I then saw a
small white cloud approaching, and when just before me, out of it came my twin sister, dressed in
white and covered with bright silver ornaments;
her long black hair, which I had often braided, fell
down her back. She clasped me round the neck
and said, 'Coacouchee! Coacouchee!' I shook
with fear. I knew her voice, but could not speak.
With one hand she gave me a string of white
beads, in the other she held a cup sparkling with
pure water. As I drank she sang the peace song
of the Seminoles and danced round me. She had
silver bells on her feet, which made a loud, sweet
noise. Taking from her bosom something, she
laid it before me, when a bright blaze streamed
above us. She took me by the hand and said,
'All here is peace!' I wanted to ask for others,
but she shook her head, stepped into the cloud,
and was gone. All was silent. I felt myself
sinking until I reached the earth, when I met my
brother Chilka. He had been seeking me, and
was alarmed at my absence."

Coacouchee fondly believed in the reality of this
vision. He declares that he lost the "white beads"
in the St. Augustine prison-chamber. It is a pity
they cannot be shown as trophies at the present
time.

His subsequent history was not unworthy of
his previous career.

The same officer who had struck off his chains at Tampa Bay and seen him safely landed in his new home in Arkansas, chanced, in the course of his duty years afterward, to be quartered upon the Mexican frontier.

One morning, happening to look out from his tent at day break, he was astonished and somewhat alarmed to see a cloud in the distance which looked like a body of armed men; the sun's first rays caught the glitter of steel. Summoning his orderly, the officer rode to the crest of a hill, in order to obtain a better view of the enemy, if such it was. Here he saw a single horseman advancing bearing a white flag. This man stated that his commander wished for an interview with the General. Presently who should ride up but the Indian warrior chief Coacouchee. He was partly, but only partly, transformed into a Mexican officer. He had commenced his habiliments from the top; he had donned a plumed hat and military full-dress long-tailed coat, with sword and epaulettes. Then he considered he had condecended far enough to civilization, and the rest of his person was still in the natural "state of the red Indian."

Poor Coacouchee! as Burns said of "Cutter Sark's garment,"

"Though in longitude t'was sorely scanty,
It was his best, and he was vaunty."

He met his old enemy and friend with affectionate welcome, and upon equal terms, for he was decorated with the insignia of a Colonel in the Mexican service.

He seemed delighted to prove to his former captor that he was a great chief in spite of those irons they had placed upon him, and pointed to the band of warriors under his command with exultation and pride.

## AS A WINTER RESORT,

St. Augustine is one of the most eligible and attractive places within the limits of the United States, especially for certain classes of invalids needing a mild and genial climate.

The air is ever balmy, yet fresh and bracing, there being more or less wind every day, and devoid of that moist, oppressive heat which visitors find so enervating upon the river. There is a large bath-house built out in the bay for the accommodation of guests, and is quite a rendezvous for young ladies in the evenings, which are always cool, and, we might almost say, always moonlight. But the fact is, that the very smallest portion of moon, which in other climates we should fail to notice, here gives so brilliant a light that it is really light two-thirds of the month. Save on the Bay of Naples I never saw the moon appear so large. The planet Venus was unusually large and brilliant, with a pale halo round it, giving a light as though it were fast

growing up a young moon itself. It is no wonder
that swimming in these silvered blue waters be-
comes the favorite fashion of the belles of Augustine, and there are few cities which can boast of
a fairer display of beauty. Being for the most
part of Spanish descent, they retain something of
the dark, flashing eye and much of the grace of
carriage; they are also particularly neat dressers,
and among the older ladies the practice of wearing black veils over the head is still prevalent, and
also the inevitable fan at all times and seasons.
Even in church the congregation keep up a soft
flutter with the motion of these fans, like the
rustle of trees by the wind.

Every vegetable, fruit and flower can be cultivated here with the least amount of labor.
Oranges could be as plentiful as apples in Here-
fordshire or peaches in Georgia, if cultivated with
the same care. Lemons, sour oranges, and the
bitter-sweet grow wild and form a most delicious
tonic drink, nearly equal to quinine for giving an
appetite. It is quite free from chills and fever,
the scourge of the South, and the summer is
equally healthy with the winter, and not so hot
as other places north or south, except the moun-
tainous regions. The same want of energy and am-
bition is observable here as in most Southern
cities. The same reason is invariably given—
"the war." Before the war every thing must,
from all accounts, have been in a state of perfec-

tion. But the whole South is in a terribly dilap-
idated condition at present. What with the four
years' ravages of war, the six years' ravages of
neglect, and the century of Southern laxity and
negro laziness, the South is almost as wild and
uncultivated as though it had only been settled a
couple of years instead of a couple of centuries.

St. Augustine must have retrograded considerably in this respect. It is stated that the city
in the time of the Spaniards was beautifully kept.
No wheeled vehicle was allowed to enter inside
the gates, which are of stone, handsomely built,
and carved in the Moorish style, containing sentry
boxes in their thickness. The streets were all
paved with the coquina, and kept so clean that
ladies used to walk out to their evening entertain-
ments in their silk slippers. Now, the streets are
ankle deep in sand, the former beautiful pavement
lying still many feet deep beneath. The sea has
gradually washed up the sand, and this failing to be
moved regularly, no trace of the pavement now remains. Sometimes after heavy rains it will leave
great holes, deep enough to bury a man if he got in.
Then, the authorities *mend* the road very much in
the Turkish fashion, viz., by making it worse. In
the latter country they mend the road by having
all the points of the stones upwards, and the
usual flattened part down. Here they have a
diabolical way of filling these holes with enormous oyster shells, which they never take the small-

est trouble to crush or break, so that you would feel yourself quite as comfortable in a rat-trap as stepping in amongst them. The streets are so narrow that the poor horses can barely find room to pass without going over this ordeal of rough oyster shells, and their hocks and feet get terribly lacerated.

There is no excuse here for not having a good pavement, as the coquina is at hand, and the streets merely require to be paved with it to make walking perfectly agreable instead of a disastrous punishment. Either your shoes are filled with sand, or your ankles scraped with oyster shells.

There are still to be seen the remains of some handsome buildings. The remains of the Treasury show signs of architectural taste, as also the queer old residence of the Governor, and the old Cathedral, picturesque from its Moorish façade and belfry. But it is probable that many of the best buildings were burnt and destroyed from time to time. The gates are the most perfect, and the fort, all of which have architectural merit. The ruins of these gates are quite a treasure to the artist; and there are many other good points for sketching and making small pictures in St. Augustine.

Photographs have been taken of numerous portions of the city, and are eagerly bought by visitors. But the great disadvantage of photography, for this kind of picture, is that it fails to convey the wonderfully beautiful gray coloring

which time and climate has lent, and destroys the
peculiar ancient appearance of the buildings, and
transforms them into the unpoetical, fresh, new
building of America. There are many pleasant
rides and drives round St. Augustine, along
the hard sand beach.

St. Augustine is somewhat of a *cul-de-sac*—
the end of creation in that direction, and to get
back into the world at large you must return
the way you came—for there is no exit elsewhere
—*via* Picolata and the St. Johns river, or by land
to Jacksonville by the road (now a mere sand
track) made by the English Governor when in
possession of Florida. The river steamers never
come to St. Augustine unless to bring or take
away troops, for in common with all other Southern cities since the war, it is garrisoned with
troops, which has the effect, at least, *pro. tem.*, of
preventing the inhabitants from expiring of
inanition. They also bring a little money into the
place, which is greatly needed, the inhabitants
being for the most part in a wretchedly poor condition, possessing no money, but heaps of Con-
federate bonds, which are not useful even to light
fires, where the pine wood will blaze up without
paper. They are, in many instances, literally
penniless, more especially the best people of the
country and in many small towns in the South.
There is a system of borrowing and lending and
bartering carried on quite amusing if it were not

too sad. There exists a listless apathy, a morbid inertness, as of people who had expended their last effort—a hopeless feeling very terrible to behold, hanging over most of the Southern cities. They are crushed, broken, ruined, and humiliated, if a people so proud can ever realize that sentiment.

Saint Augustine is not only unique for its peculiar antiquity, but it possesses a speciality of its own, for it can boast of a manufacture peculiar to itself. Small and insignificant as it is, it is the only town in this country we have visited which has a speciality.* In England most towns have, or have had, a special manufacture of their own. As Sheffield for cutlery, Coventry for ribbons, Nottingham for lace, Matlock for its spar and marble ornaments, Tunbridge for its wood-carving —every town, almost, is celebrated for something. St. Augustine is thus celebrated for making hats, baskets, fans and boxes, out of the palmetto—very pretty and fanciful—and no strangers leave the place without carrying away some little souvenir. They also make baskets and mats of the strong wire-grass, which are quite durable and useful. The old-fashioned Spanish lace-making is the prominent needle-work among the inhabitants, but is not of the best style, and is very tedious and trying to the eyes.

* The author had evidently made a very limited examination of the United States when this remark was written.

Recently some French nuns have arrived from Le Puys, in France, brought over for the instruction of the poor black as well as white, by the energetic Bishop of Savannah. They come from that part of France where the beautiful thread and silk lace is made, such as Cluney, Passementerie, Guissure, Valenciennes and Lille. They are proficients in their art, and in their own country devoted their lives to instructing the poor in religion, a simple education, and the means of earning their own living, by teaching them to make lace. They open large work-rooms where, after the children have gone through their exercises of reading and writing, they are each supplied with a little frame or cushion, thread and bobbins, and they are taught lace-making for the rest of the day. A child of eight years old can learn it, and can be taught as early as they could be taught their notes on the piano, and little girls take a great delight in it, especially in making trimming for their dolls, and the first communion veil. In that part of France every woman and child, rich and poor, knows how to make lace. When visiting that part of France three years ago, we all took the mania, and commenced cushion lace-making with great vigor. It is very interesting work, and the satisfaction great in wearing lace of your own manufacture. Ladies all make it for pastime, and the poor for profit. Old women almost blind and bedridden can still continue making the same pattern they have done all their lives, and earn enough to keep themselves in a tidy little room until they go to a better habitation. If the sisters could succeed in establishing the same work and class-rooms in St. Augustine, there is no reason why it should not speedily rival Ciuny or Valenciennes. There are a number of young persons in this ancient Spanish city who are peculiarly adapted to this work from their domestic habits, refusing to leave home for any service, but having ingenuity and adaptability of finger. These girls, if they were taught, could make rapid fortunes for themselves and their quaint and beautiful little city. Not a yard of lace worn by any lady on this great continent which is not imported, and half a dozen profits levied therefor, besides the duty, before she can touch it. Girls working it at home, at no expense but the raw material, which is trifling, could sell it, making a handsome profit, at less than two-thirds the price paid for it at present in this country. In Malta, where the young girls all make lace, and are very similar in habits and character to the St. Augustinians, we bought rich black silk lace (in wear ever since, five years) for exactly one-third of what it is valued at in America; for the reason that here, after it leaves the hands of the girl who makes it, it passes through those of half a dozen buyers, sellers, agents, merchants, custom-house and store-keepers. The greatest

lace manufactories have been started by one or
two persons having the art, and settling down in
a spot. The object of the sisters is simply to do
good to their fellows. They have devoted their
lives to charity in any and every shape and form,
whether it be teaching the ignorant, tending the
sick, soothing the miserable, teaching God's word,
or teaching the needy to earn their bread, and
thus putting them above temptation; they are
but fulfilling their vocation of charity. And so
much respect do I bear to these devoted sisters
of charity, whom I have known as a body since I
was four years old, that I cheerfully take this opportunity of testifying to their great merit, and
trust, with all my heart, that their good works
may be crowned with success in this world, as
their earnest, devoted endeavor will surely be
crowned hereafter.

The hats are made by slitting and plait-
ing the palmetto, which when completed resembles very much the coarse straw hats of other
countries, being lighter or whiter, or it is said, not
cleanable. But the ornaments with which they
trim them constitute the beauty of the hat. The
broad, smooth palmetto leaf is cut into various
forms of leaves and flowers and feathers, and resembles the finest Swiss wood work; frequently
the sugar-cane flower is added as a feather, and
imitates a golden Maraborie. The trimming is in
fact the whole charm of the hat. The ornamen-

tation upon fans, boxes, watch-pockets, and a variety of small articles, is also very tasteful and peculiar, and displays a talent and ingenuity remarkable only as a generality in this little spot of the Southern States, where there appears rather a lack of original inventiveness. Other hats are made from a strong grass called the wire-grass, which when stitched with colored silk have a very pretty effect, and are exceedingly durable. Mats and all kinds of baskets are made of the same wire-grass, and resemble in appearance, strength and durability the baskets made by the Arabs in Algiers, on the coast of Africa. The manufacture is so similar that it would lead one to suppose that the Augustinans learned it from the Spaniards, who took it from the Moors in Spain, who brought it from Tunis and the African coast—a curious history for a basket.

There is little doubt that St. Augustine will eventually become as fashionable a resort as West Point, Newport, or Saratoga, and more vitally important than any of the above-named places, on account of its life-giving properties to all persons afflicted with pulmonary disease, and all maladies which require a mild and equable climate. Pleasant summer resorts are rarely suitable for winter residences, and many families and individuals find it too inconvenient and expensive to change their abode twice a year. The moving of all one's belongings, and the packing up of household gods,

is often a consideration that weighs to keep many
a poor invalid in a climate which every day saps
the fountain of his life, which in a genial atmosphere might flow on softly for a number of years.

It is no uncommon case for consumptives to
live for ten or fifteen years with but one lung, in
a climate such as St. Augustine, where no bitter
eastern wind ever irritates the remaining lung,
where no biting frost ever congests the respiratory
organs the year round, where the summer knows
no enervating heat, or the winter any intense cold,
but glide imperceptibly into each other, wafted in
and out by a clear sea breeze, not keen enough to
chill the most sensitive, but cool enough to be a
grateful fan.

Fully realizing these great advantages, numerous wealthy families from the North have established themselves permanently at St. Augustine,
where they live the year round, in great comfort
and considerable elegance, which the climate
permits; going on pleasure-trips only for amusement and relaxation of change. Their houses are
unsurpassed, for luxury and convenience, by any
thing in the States. Commanding piazzas, inter-
laced with gorgeous flowery creepers and vines;
hanging baskets of drooping moss and lichens;
shady walks beneath the orange and magnolia;
fine airy rooms, catching the balmy gale of the
citron from one side or the other. There is always
one side of the house where, in the height of

summer it is quite cool. There is the advantage of excellent fishing, and for gentlemen who are given to sporting, there is an abundance of game—wild turkey, wild duck, deer, bear, and smaller game; oysters in plenty, crabs, mullet, sheepshead, and others in great variety. It is almost needless to say, that vegetables can be grown in the greatest profusion and variety, and through the whole season—peas in January, and tomatoes in March.

Many northern families not only grow all their own fruits and vegetables, but have such an exceeding quantity, that they easily supply the tables of various hotels and boarding-houses in St. Augustine, which are usually full of visitors in the winter months.

Of these, the Magnolia House, kept by Mrs. Buffington, is a spacious, clean, commodious house, with snug, airy rooms opening on to a wide balcony or veranda, overhanging a quaint old-fashioned garden, the walks marked out by coquina stone, reminding one of some old cloister garden in monastic enclosures. It is ever flowery the year round with perfumed orange blossoms, scarlet pomegranate, yellow chaporelle, pink, crape, myrtle, and a variety of other blooming trees, gladening the eyes of the weary invalid with their cool, fragrant beauty. On the other side of the garden, in a green field well shaded with trees, is an old-fashioned Methodist chapel, from whence, early on Sabbath morning, comes wafted the

sweet voice of young children, singing their
Sunday school hymn, "The river, the beautiful
river, that flows by the throne of God." So gold-
en floods the light over this scene, so deliciously
perfumed is the air these Sunday mornings, so
holy and benignant is all around, so sacredly all
nature seems to join with the heavens in "telling
the glory of God," that could one be sure there
was "peace and good will among men," it would
not be difficult to believe that this in truth was
the promised land the little children are singing of.
There is also a Presbyterian church, and the minister, like most of his brethren of that denomina-
tion, delivers a sound, sterling, excellent discourse
twice every Sunday.

Besides these is the Roman Catholic church,
on the Plaza, already described, with the Moorish
belfry; and the Episcopal church, whose amiable
and intelligent minister resides at the Magnolia.
Also a Baptist assembly of negroes, which it is
worth any stranger's while to visit, if they wish to
form a correct idea of how far Christianity has
permeated into some of these dark skins.

There are two convents for the education of
all classes—black and white, rich and poor; for
these devoted Sisters rarely do any thing by
halves.

To Catholic families, with delicate girls re-
quiring a warm climate and tender care, as well
as education, this convent—which is a handsome

building, surrounded by a large garden—offers considerable advantages rarely to be met with in a school. There are a number of French Sisters from whom they would have all the facility of learning the language, together with all the usual branches of an English education.

To those girls whose future livelihood depended upon their own exertion, the lace-making would prove a valuable acquirement; for a girl able to work this lace can earn from four to five dollars a day—sitting quietly in her own room, with her little cushion before her—with half the exertion of playing the piano. The St. Augustine girls excel, as we have shown, in ingenuity of fingers practised by Europeans.

Every Frenchwoman is a superior needle woman, and their fancy-work of all descriptions is spread over the whole world.

Germans are wonderful knitters, wool-workers, and toy makers.

The Swiss—ivory-carvers and wood-cutters.

The Italians — mosaic-setters in stone and wood, cameo and coral-carvers.

The Armenian Turkish woman's embroidery in gold, silk, and pearls, excels the whole world.

In America there is little of this ingenuity of finger, unless in St. Augustine,* where it is prominent, and is destined to take rank with any European continental city; for the same genius is

* Probably the writer's observation has been rather limited.

4

noticeable, the same gift is innate to the people, and will sooner or later display itself in its own way.

Some little incident to quicken the impetus, and St. Augustine may rise like a Phœnix from the ashes and blood which centuries of war have heaped upon her devoted head. America is a living marvel for the rapid rise of her new cities; but her old ones need not crumble into dust for all that—and such is not the fate of her oldest. She will yet stand with pride among her children and great-great-grandchildren cities—such as Chicago—as alert and juvenile as any, only shaking her hoary locks, as old folks will, over her long experience and wisdom.

There is a large garrison kept in this city, which tends largely to support and enliven the place by the daily performance of the military band, which plays alternately upon the Plaza, in the evening, and the barracks.

This cheery music breaks the stillness and monotony of a small town with a most exhilarating effect. The inhabitants hear the enlivening strains, and sally forth on to the Plaza. Young men and maidens, children and old persons; and of course all the negroes who can muster.

No doubt General Sprague, the commander of this district, has discovered the beneficial effect of soothing and conciliatory policy, for there is no man who has filled this very difficult and arduous post with more successful results, and who is more admired and beloved by all parties.

In some towns there are Southern ladies who will not allow their eyes to fall on a Northern epaulette, however agreable its wearer may endeavor to make himself. But a lady would have to be something more or less than a woman if she could resist or fail to appreciate the nobility and benevolence which nature has stamped upon the countenance of Col. Sprague, and the effect is manifest. Surrounded by a charming family, his house is hospitably open to all the best people visiting St. Augustine.

The house itself is a most interesting object, from its strongly marked Spanish character. From the colonnade or veranda running around it, you enter at once without hall or vestibule into a large room about fifty or sixty feet long, only broken by two Moorish archways, over which curtains can drop to form two separate rooms. The archways meeting in the centre form the fire-place, back and front, for each side of the room, whose capacious chimney, where half a dozen persons might ensconce themselves cosily, are ornamented with massive brass dog-irons, and in chilly weather a brilliant log fire completes the picture. There are eight doors to the room, all partially glass, and as the family is large and entertain all comers, the constant ingress and egress is almost like a pantomime, and render it one of

the most amusing and picturesque rooms I have
ever visited.

At door number one entered a gay-uniformed
officer, doffing plumed hat and proceeding to pay
his devoirs to a pretty girl seated in the shade of
the archway, where she seems to have expected
him. At door number two rush in such exquisite-
ly beautiful children, that one imagines they have
been made to grace this scene specially; at the
third door follows their ugly old black nurse, or
mamy; an orderly is waiting at the fourth for
commands; by the fifth enter a bevy of highly
worked up fashionable ladies from New York,
visiting Saint Augustine in order to say they have
been there. At number six appear a party of naval
officers from the cutter lying in the bay. At number seven glide quietly in two meek-looking Sisters of Charity, for all have recourse to Mrs.
Sprague in their difficulties and trouble. She is
seated on a couch near her aged mother, who has
been an invalid, and whilst bending her classical-
shaped head gracefully towards the Sisters, and
listening with a placid smile to their wants and
requirements, she watches with tender devotion
every movement of her mother. She is all thought
and feeling for every one—for all but herself.

Mrs. Sprague was one of the beautiful daugh-
ters of General Worth, celebrated in the Florida
and Mexican war; she is, therefore, thoroughly
acquainted with the temper, feeling, and senti-

ments of the South, and thus is a most valuable adjunct in this way to her husband.

St. Augustine has been fortunate in having such a military commander, and fully appreciates her good luck, for with such an open house and the people who keep it, St. Augustine could never be wanting in pleasant society.

Boating on the bay is a favorite amusement on moonlight nights, and in the day, boating excursions to gather shells on the opposite beach of the Island of Anastasia, which abounds in very beautiful ones. Collecting sea mosses and lichens, is a pleasant occupation; and for those who can arrange them scientifically, it would be possible to make a classified album, such as are made and sold by the thousand in the Isles of Wight, Jersey and Guernsey, in the old country. There are several good sailing boats for hire, and the day's amusement healthful and delightful, even tho' " the shells we gather are soon thrown idly by."

Some ladies make excursions over to the pearly white sand beach to bathe, in preference to the bathing-house immediately on Bay street.

To Americans who have not visited Europe, or only such modern portions of London, Paris, and capitals which more or less resemble New York, St. Augustine would possess a fund of interest, from its antiquities and curious appearance; for although it greatly resembles Italian, Spanish Moorish towns, it is totally unlike any thing else in America, where all is comparatively modern and new. A stranger may form a very correct idea of what Cadiz, Tunis, Terracina may be like, looking at St. Augustine, especially by moonlight, when all its defects are hidden and all its beauties enhanced. And it seems to be generally moonlight. From the fact of the great clearness of the atmosphere, the smallest portion of moon gives a very strong light; whether crescent or waning moon, it lights up the place with an astonishing vividness which I have only seen equalled on the Bay of Naples.

The star-light nights are wondrously lovely, and the myriads of fire-flies of such size and brightness, that it looks as though the stars were descending upon the earth. Heaven and earth coming together, which no doubt would be a very pleasant circumstance, if it would really happen.

But these moonlight nights are the glory of Saint Augustine. So bright and cool, and soft and balmy, few can resist the enjoyableness of a stroll, or the dreamy bliss of sitting out on the veranda listening to the echoes of the band or the tinkling of some distant guitar—dreaming over all the happiness we know, past, present, or to come.

Evening is the time for visiting, and there is a great deal of cosy neighboring amongst the townspeople. Of course it is the time for love-making, and to the delicious moonlight nights is no doubt attributable the unusual number of marriages in this place, which seems to keep the small city in a perfect flutter of anticipation and excitement.

It certainly deserves to be patronized by New England ladies, where, I understand, there is such an overplus of the gentler sex. They could not fail to find a mate under this specific of moonlight at St. Augustine. One lady, we were informed, had been married five times. It seems a great number, but we suppose she could not help it under the circumstances.

The great desideratum for St. Augustine is a railroad from thence to Picolata, so that the route would then be quite direct from New York, with only one change of steamer at Charleston or Savannah. Splendid steamers ply almost daily from New York to either of these towns, where several fine steamers continue the route up the St. Johns river to Picolata, the nearest point to St. Augustine. There are at present, stages to carry the passengers through the pine forests to St. Augustine. The ride, to a lover of nature, is charming, and not by any means monotonous. The whole distance is garlanded by flowers of every variety —lilies, honeysuckles, azelias, sunflowers, and a thousand varieties of small flowers which enamel the ground. Through forests of pine on the luxurious hummuck land of green oak magnolia, here

and there you may see the milk-white heron floating in the cloudless azure vault, looking like a
messenger angel bearing glad tidings to earth;
now and then a startled deer scudding away from
the appearance of man—and to those who can
appreciate all these beauties, the ride is delightful. But the generality of travellers are intent
upon getting there and nothing else; therefore,
a railroad would convert the eighteen miles into
nine, and an uncomfortable stage carriage into a
comfortable railroad car.

It is therefore to be hoped that very shortly
a rail for these few miles will be established, and
there is no doubt it would be a profitable venture
for Northern speculators to unite St. Augustine
with New York, with only one change, in a space
of time of four or five days; so that persons
snowed up in New York, shivering through their
furs, having their extremities pinched blue and
red, and all sorts of unbecoming colors; tor-
mented with colds in the head, bidding defiance
to troches, caudle, and Dr. Brown's lozenges, etc.,
etc.—such persons have only to put themselves
comfortably to bed in one of the excellent steamers,
take rather a long nap, and awake inhaling the
perfume of the orange blossom and the golden
fruit, hanging in rich clusters, ready to be plucked
and eaten.

Wrapped to the eyes in mufflers, the half-be-
numbed traveller pioneers his way to the steamer

wharf at New York, now over hillocks of drifted
snow, now through slushy swamps of melted
ditto; a bleak north-east wind is whistling
through the blocks of buildings, which look black
and dreary, as if they too suffered from the bitter
cold. Every one he meets is huddling himself
together to keep all the little warmth he has in
his body from escaping. The very animals stand-
ing to be burdened or unloaded, have on them a
look as if they had now once for all resigned all
hope of ever feeling comfortable again.

The steamer, when reached, is coated and
clothed and draped with ice and icicles; all her
spars are slippery with ice, her rigging and ropes
stiff and festooned in ice; she is united to every
thing round about her with ice, and when she
moves there will be a terrible smashing and
crashing and bursting asunder of icy bonds.
She looks as dreary as ever a ship can look,
and of the captain there is nothing whatever to
be seen or understood but his eyes; a great
fur cap and cape join with his beard and conceal
his nose and mouth, and a coat of similar material
disguises the rest of his person. You discover
that this furry, hairy animal is the captain, from
hearing clear, distinct orders issue from thence.
How surprised you are two days after, when you
are greeted by a pleasant, fair-faced, white waist-
coated individual, straw hat in hand, "Fine day,
ma'am; making sixteen knots," and find it to be

the captain come out of his shell or rather his furry skin. You, too, have done the same if you had one, and are watching the porpoises play and bask in the sun, running in past the famous Fort Sumter at Charleston, where the roses hang heavy on their stems, and where you are soon eating pineapple and mangoes. Any one who has experienced this rapid contrast will never forget the delight of the sensation, the sudden relief from wearisome precautions against cold—the speedy exit of the enemy who has held us in durance vile and siege of his bitter fangs for so long; of the release of the respiratory organs, which begin to exert their functions without a conscious effort; of the feeling of exhilaration and happiness, and the bound of enjoyment which transports the whole existence.

This rapid change of climate from mid-winter in New York to Florida, is one of the most astonishing effects of steam. We know the enormous distance we have come from the change in the atmosphere, and thus realize the annihilation of space by science. This short space of rail from St. Augustine to Picolata, would enable her to send her early fruits and vegetables to New York and other northern towns, in the same manner as Jacksonville and Fernandina, at least six weeks earlier,—peas, potatoes, tomatoes, grapes, oranges, cucumbers, and every vegetable which will bear carriage. England is supplied in this way from

France, Holland, Belgium, with fruit and vegetables, a month earlier than she can produce them;
and there is a much greater eagerness to possess
things in a hurry in America, than England. The
northern cities of America would pay any price
to obtain any thing a little before the natural
course of time — in fact, to "hurry up" the
seasons.

In speaking of Florida as a slip of land projecting from the American continent, it will be
curious to English readers to know that Florida
is about the exact length and breadth of England
and Scotland, together! with a magnificent river,
the St. Johns, flowing through the length, for
about three hundred miles, when it is met by the
Indian river; thus forming a national high-road
through the rich and luxuriant country.

A great river is one of the greatest blessings
to a new country. It is the "providential high-
way," which needs no macadamizing; a railroad,
without the trouble of laying down the rails. It
also supplies rations gratis in its fish. In the St.
Johns is splendid fishing for bass, cat-fish, perch,
and other fish. Wild fowl abound. The stately
pelican floats on its broad waters, and the sea-gulls
skim the air.

# ADDENDA.

From New York, travellers have the choice of three conveyances, viz.:

I. *Railroad*, via Washington, Richmond, and Charleston or Savannah; and thence by steamer to St. Johns River: or railroad direct to Jacksonville, Florida.

II. By steamer to CHARLESTON; and thence by the St. Johns River steamers to Jacksonville and Picolata, via Savannah. Fare to Charleston, $15. *Through tickets* to Picolata may be obtained at a cheaper rate.

N. B.—In this way the traveller has the advantage of seeing Charleston and its surroundings, and of resting there perhaps one or two days.

III. By steamer to SAVANNAH; and thence by the same line of Florida steamers as from Charleston—as they touch at Savannah. There are two lines, so that there is a steamer every other day. Livingston Fox & Co., 88 Liberty street, are the agents.

The steamers now running from Charleston to East Florida via Savannah, Fernandina, Jacksonville to Palatka, are the City Point and Dictator; and those from Savannah are the Lizzy Baker and St. Mary's. All of these boats are of good size with all the comfort of the North River steamers of New York.

The fare to Palatka, the head of navigation for these steamers, from Savannah is about $10. From Charleston $15.

The route from the Northern States to Florida is not at all difficult. One can take a steamship every other day in the week from the city of New York direct to Savannah or Charleston and then continue the journey to East Florida on a smaller class of steamers. Through tickets can be purchased in New York to Palatka on the St. Johns River for $33$\frac{75}{100}$. Five days time is sufficient to finish the journey. Or if any one desires to take a land route, through tickets can be obtained from New York by rail to Jacksonville ; where the Savannah and Charleston steamers call two or three times a week, to land and receive passengers for St. Johns River.

To reach St. Augustine, through tickets should be purchased to Picolata, and from thence take the stage 18 miles at a cost of $3 or $4 to the ancient city.

The largest town on the St. Johns River is Jacksonville, which is located some 25 miles above the mouth, and the next town of importance is Palatka, a very pleasant place about 65 miles south of the former.

Enterprise is considered the head of navigation for St. Johns River steamboats, and is about 200 miles from the mouth of the river. The fare from Jacksonville to enterprise is about $7. (Two boats a week, via. Palatka.)

The Magnolia House and the Florida House are the principal hotels at St. Augustine, and these are moderately comfortable—charges from $15 per week ; but the are a number of fairly kept boarding-houses in the place, which are well patronized by strangers during the winter season. Essential improvements in the hotels are promised for the season of 1868--9. The Florida House is to be in charge of a host who "knows how to keep a hotel," from a northern city.

At Jacksonville there are a number of hotels, and they have just got a charter from the legislature to build one on a large scale.

At Palatka there is a population of about 1,000 ; and they also have a charter for an extensive hotel and park. There are two large hotels, the Putnam House, and St. Johns House, both of which have the reputation of being as well kept as any hotels in the South. This place is famous for orange-groves.

At Enterprise there is a large hotel which is handsomely situated on the Lake Shore. There is a hotel at Hibernia, and one at Green Cove Spring, both being romantic situations on the bank of the River St. Johns between Jacksonville and Palatka.

The prices of board at all the public and private houses named, range from $8 to $25 per week.

The colored population in the Eastern part of the State and in the towns mentioned, is quite small compared to other parts of the South, for the reason that the St. Johns River country is newly settled, the lands bordering on its banks not being suitable for the culture of cotton, and only adapted to the cultivation of vegetables and fruit. Hence, of late there has been almost a mania for orange groves, and now there can be seen thousands of orange trees recently planted out on the river, by Northern as well as Southern settlers, all of whom seem to toil side by side, and try to forget, in the charms of the climate and amidst their beautiful groves, that there had ever been trouble between their respective sections of country.

No Northern visitor to Florida should fail to make the round trip up the St. John's River, as far as Enterprise.

Invalids returning North should graduate the change of climate by stopping for a time at Aiken, S. C.

×

www.ingramcontent.com/pod-product-compliance
Lightning Source LLC
Chambersburg PA
CBHW021530090426
42739CB00007B/858